The Key Adult in School

THE ATTACHMENT AWARE SCHOOL SERIES
Bridging the gap for troubled pupils

Book 1   The Key Adult in School
Book 2   The Senior Manager in School
Book 3   The Key Teacher in School
Book 4   The Team Pupil in School
Book 5   The Parent and Carer in School

**Other books in the
Attachment Aware Schools Collection®**

ATTACHMENT AWARE SCHOOLS COLLECTION®

Attachment in the Classroom
Better Play
Conversations That Matter
Inside I'm Hurting
Little-Mouse Finds a Safe Place
School as a Secure Base
Settling to Learn
Teaching the Unteachable
Teenagers and Attachment
Temper Temper!
What About Me?
What Can I Do With The Kid Who…?
You think I'm Evil

ATTACHMENT AWARE SCHOOL SERIES

Bridging the gap for troubled pupils

Book 1

The Key Adult in School

Louise Michelle Bombèr

Worth Publishing

First published 2015 by Worth Publishing Ltd
worthpublishing.com

© Worth Publishing Ltd 2015
Reprinted 2016

All rights reserved. No part of this publication may be reproduced, stored in a retrieval system or transmitted in any form, or by any means, electronic, mechanical, photocopying, recording or otherwise, without the prior permission of the publishers, nor be otherwise circulated without the publisher's consent in any form of binding or cover other than that in which it is published and without a similar condition being imposed on the subsequent purchaser.

Printed and bound by CPI Group (UK) Ltd., Croydon CR0 4YY

British Library Cataloguing in Publication Data
A catalogue record for this book is available from the British Library
ISBN   9781903269282

Cover and text design by Anna Murphy

For Jane Airey,
who played a significant role
in my journey

Biography

Louise Michelle Bombèr is a specialist Attachment Lead Teacher and a therapist. She has worked for many years with children and young people who have experienced significant relational traumas and losses. Working in many different contexts she is passionate about ensuring these pupils have opportunity to adapt and recover so that they can make the most of all that school offers. She continues to work as a practitioner using Theraplay®, PACE, DDP and sensory interventions to support children and their parents.

Louise is the author of *Inside I'm Hurting*, *What About Me?*, co-author with Dr Dan Hughes of *Settling to Learn* and contributor to *Teenagers and Attachment*. Her work has been greatly influenced by John Bowlby, Dan Hughes, Daniel Siegel, Bruce Perry and Gabor Maté. Louise advises, trains and supports education professionals and families, and is involved in direct work with children and young people in class, in the therapy room and at an allotment project, PLOT 22 (*and see* touchbase.org.uk). She heads up a network which enables Attachment Leads to be trained to provide advocacy and support in individual schools across the UK (attachmentleadnetwork.net).

Acknowledgements

Thanks to Dr Kim Golding for her continued partnership with me, and my long standing supervisor Penny Auton, who has walked alongside me in my professional journey over many, many years. I would like to thank Jenny Peters in the UK and Glen Cooper in the USA for generously providing me with commentary on Circle of Security®, which is such an invaluable resource to all those wanting to make a difference in children's lives.

I would like to honour all those parents and carers that have shared their stories so vulnerably with me over the years as to what it is like to parent these children. I admire you and so wish that your children could see what I see, how much you deeply love them and root for them and how you desire for them to know how much they are valued, special and that they 'belong' to your family. This is so hard for them to take in.

My current TouchBase™ team - Jennie Fellows, Julia Wilde, Keeley de Freese, Becs Uvieghara, Natalie Miller, Tania Druce,

Alice Mallorie and Henrietta Kuhudzai for your dedication and commitment to these children; it doesn't go unnoticed. My national trainers, Anne Henderson, Clare Langhorne, Alison Lumley, Helen Wallace and Helen Wright who so passionately deliver materials they believe in, whilst continuing as practitioners actively involved with many pupils. All the support assistants and mentors with whom I have journeyed since 2000; together we have learned what is needed.

My editor and friend Andrea Perry who encourages and mobilises me into further creativity. My husband Jonathan Fordham, who often releases me from household responsibilities because he believes in this cause as much as I do. Thanks for holding the fort when I bury my head in books and my laptop! Lucinda and Steve Smith who lead with both gentleness and strength, continuing to be really behind my vision to see dignity restored. Nothing goes unnoticed.

All the brave families who have endured more than many will ever know and yet remain standing clothed in dignity and strength and armed with fierce compassion for their hurting children. May this series of books play some part in raising much needed awareness so that you can take a step back, trusting the schools your children attend to nurture them into all they should have been first time around.

Foreword

Children with relational trauma and loss have particular vulnerabilities that can make attending school difficult. Attachment aware schools are healthy for all, but essential for these most vulnerable of pupils. Integral to this is the Key Adult. This person has a pivotal and direct role with the pupil, backed up and supported by the rest of the team.

We must not underestimate how challenging it is to offer relationship experience to pupils with relational traumas in their lives. This challenge can be represented by one word: 'fear'. Pupils fear relationship, fear connection, fear being understood. They do not trust that they can be accepted unconditionally; they do not believe that connection will be good for them. They experience high levels of shame, believing they are not worthy of what is being offered to them, and they have learnt to deal with this fear by miscuing the adults around them, hiding what they most need. Key Adults have to understand this challenge if they are to help the pupil overcome their fears and enter into relationship with them. Only then can the school work for the pupil.

Louise's **Attachment Aware School Series** will be an important addition to the support that the Team around the pupil needs when helping those with relational traumas. Within this Team none is more central to providing such support than the Key Adult. Key Adults need resilience, confidence and guidance to fulfil their role. In *The Key Adult in School*, Louise's experience and wisdom shine through as she provides practical, clear and inspiring advice to support Key Adults in this most challenging of tasks. Within these pages, those working as Key Adults in schools will find help to understand the role, and practical advice to fulfil it. They will gain in confidence to become an important part of the Team, supporting and advocating for the child. The self-reflection that forms an important part of the advice that Louise gives will additionally help the reader to grow and develop as a relational adult, leading to benefits both within and outside of school.

This book provides an essential resource, contributing to the resilience that Key Adults will need if they are to provide the relational support that the pupils cannot manage without, but will resist because of their core fears. Overcoming the fear and providing relationship will make a significant difference to the pupils' progress in school.

Kim S Golding, 2015

Contents

Introduction 1

PART 1	**Becoming a Key Adult**	**9**
	Ideal qualities of a Key Adult	12
	Core aims of the Key Adult-Key Pupil relationship	13
	Good questions about Key Adults	14
PART 2	**The Key Adult and the Team Around the Child: Team Pupil**	**17**
	Responsibilities of Key Adults	22
	10 things Key Adults say to encourage anyone new taking up this role	25

continues/...

PART 3	**So – let's get going!**	**27**
	A Know your own story	29
	EXERCISES to build self-awareness	33
	B Manage your stress	48
	STRESS PLAN (1)	56
	preventative plan outside work	
	STRESS PLAN (2) preventative plan at work	59
	CRISIS PLAN AT WORK	62
	10 pieces of advice from experienced Key Adults	64
	C Know your role	65
	D Know your pupil - and bring yourself to the relationship	72
	E Advocacy - when things go wrong	79
	10 things that other people in Team Pupil say about Key Adults	84
Glossary		87
References		94
Useful contatcs		99

Introduction

This pocket-sized book is part of the **Attachment Aware School Series**. The series has come about in response to an increasing understanding that security, through the experience of safe and atuned relationships, is necessary for every pupil to be able to settle to learn and make the most of all the educational opportunities out there. It is only when a pupil's **attachment system** is attended to that their **exploratory system** can really come into play.

Some children may have learned security outside school through their experience of relationships to date - others may not. Some pupils find settling into learning incredibly difficult, especially those who have a history of not being attended to, or responded to sufficiently, or often enough; of neglect, traumatic experience or significant loss. If circumstances have ruptured or inhibited the development of an internal, felt sense of security, then children often experience huge anxiety - sometimes unnoted by those of us observing.

The Key Adult in School

These pupils are not in a position to learn or take up the huge range of opportunities available to them in school YET. So in school, we must first address their need for security and stability - by providing them with a consistent, reliable, empathic, attuned attachment relationship in school. Only then can we expect them to make progress with learning, and to fully engage with school life.

On really difficult days, even the most securely attached child - or adult - may find learning a struggle. So this series of pocket books endorses the view that if a school is fully attachment aware and indeed trauma informed (*see later*) *all pupils and staff will benefit*. Ideally all staff will have attachment aware training as their foundation, and with this background will appreciate that for some pupils a specific, targeted relational intervention will be a life-line.

In the **Attachment Aware School Series** we advocate having a small tight team around these specific pupils - Team Pupil. So, in school we will have Team Lee, Team Grace, Team Aiden ... four or five people in different positions of responsibility in the school. All believing *in* and rooting *for* the pupil.

> Having several good attachment relationships predicts better self-control, behaviour and relationships.
> Belsky et al 2007

In the primary phase, this team will usually be made up of the **Key Adult**, the class teacher, the SENCO or INCO, the Assistant Head and the Head. In the secondary phase, this would usually be the **Key Adult**, the form tutor, the Head of Year, the SENCO/INCO and the Assistant Head. In addition to this school-based team, each pupil needs to know that their parents or carers are on board in their education, trusting those involved to support their child and actively working in tight partnership within their unique team.

With this in mind, there are five books in the **Attachment Aware School Series**, each reflecting the different roles of the different individuals in the team around the pupil (one pocket book for each member of the team). The series is written to help this valuable community work well together and hold the pupil in mind, shoring the pupil up when necessary, serving as an anchor so that anxieties can be relieved; freeing up the possibility for this child or young person to become all they were intended to become, first time around. I have also included a pocket book for the parents or carers of the pupil, since they will be and often are valuable contributors to the school team.

Throughout each book you'll find some key terms are highlighted in **bold**: you'll find all of these in the Glossary on p.87.

The Key Adult in School

This particular book is intended for those who have been assigned the role of the **Key Adult** for a troubled pupil at school.

Key Adults are usually members of support staff - teaching assistants (TAs), individual needs assistants (INAs), emotional literacy support assistants (ELSAs) or mentors from the main school staff within a school. **Key Adults** prepare themselves to be the best **additional attachment figures** they can be for those pupils who have experienced toxic stress from pregnancy onwards, and/or have had compromised or **disrupted relationships/connections** with adults in their early years.

We now know that a history of **relational trauma and loss** needn't be a life sentence of insecure attachments, **developmental vulnerabilities**, low educational outcomes and a compromised future. Children and young people *can* learn security and can negotiate and consolidate the necessary developmental milestones. But they need us all alongside them to do so.

Education from 5 to 16 is compulsory in the UK, and so these children and young people will be with us for many weeks, terms and years. If they have been wounded '*within relationship,*' it makes sense for us to prioritise and use quality relational interventions to help them, as *relationship* is the necessary vehicle for supporting adaption and recovery.

> For many children and young people, a sense of connectedness with just one adult ... is enough to end their deep sense of aloneness, isolation, not belonging, not being understood.
>
> Sunderland 2015, p.19

We know now that both emotional growth and well-being are directly linked to learning. We also know that the more a child or young person experiences quality connections with mature adults, the more mature his brain becomes.

So it is our professional responsibility to invest time and resources into facilitating relationally rich contexts for this particular group of pupils with challenging histories of relational trauma and loss.

We also know from neuroscience that the richer *relational experiences* these pupils have, the more complex the neural pathways and connections in their brains will be, meaning that relationships bring integration. Integration brings health - physical, mental and emotional health. And richer relational experiences and more complex systems in the brain mean the pupil will be able to engage in more complex thinking, relating and being. This is the way ahead for all of us who take our pupils' well-being and development seriously.

The Key Adult in School

> Let's shift from a behavioural view of pupils to a relational one - focussing on trying to understand what their behaviour means [or communicates].
>
> Hughes & Baylin 2012, p.8 (*my parantheses*)

Up until recently, it was thought that the responsibility to support the mental health and well-being of these children and young people lay solely with their parents/carers, social workers and therapists. However, I know first-hand from many years of experience out in schools how powerful a **Key Adult** relationship and an assigned Team Pupil can be within the educational context.

Key Adults who are physically and emotionally present, attentive, attuned and responsive, provide the ground for these children and young people to thrive. And those **Key Adults** who also employ *playfulness*, communicate *acceptance*, engage *curiosity* and show *empathy* (PACE, Hughes, 2009), *and see below* p.73) can actually support these children and young people into new learning, development and opportunities. The possibilities are endless!

> Teacher-student attunement is not a 'nice addition' to the learning experience but a core requirement.
>
> Cozolino 2013, p.18

To make the best use of this book, your whole school community would first ideally have had at least two full days of training in child development, attachment, neuroscience, and trauma to create a platform for effective, consistent, attachment aware practice in school. All these key principles and practices will obviously need to be re-visited on a regular basis in order to truly embed the work I'll be outlining in this book (and throughout the **Attachment Aware School Series**) into the usual ways of how we are and what we do within the school culture.

In addition, I recommend that each school allocates an interested member of support staff and senior management to train up as Attachment Leads so that they can ensure quality practice, and keep the momentum going (*see* attachmentleadnetwork.net).

A NOTE ABOUT CONSULTATION

Each of us needs to be clear as to the boundaries of our role and responsibilities. There are occasions when attachment aware interventions will not be sufficient, and a trauma informed practitioner will need to be involved for specialist assessments, advice and interventions (*and see the pocket book in this Series,* Team Pupil pp.39-41).

Who should that individual be? I would strongly recommend a specialist therapist with complex trauma/ **developmental trauma** expertise. Our children and young people need appropriate professionals involved who

The Key Adult in School

will provide an extension to the ground work already laid down within the attachment aware practices employed by a school. This is our joint ethical responsibility. As well as detailed assessments and direct interventions, these same professionals can also provide specialist supervision to staff in school on a regular basis. Increasing staff care increases our care-giving capacity, which means that we will then be more able to facilitate the permanency that our pupils need. By facilitating and honouring the vehicle of relationship, we will be 'respecting biology' (Perry, 2014).

Let the quality connections begin!

Please note: In this book I reference material from my earlier publications, using acronyms for their titles for accessibility. These books form a key resource for developing attachment awareness and trauma informed interventions in schools, and provide background reading for the **Attachment Aware School Series.**

Inside I'm Hurting	(2007)	**(IIH)**
What About Me?	(2011)	**(WAM)**
Settling to Learn (with Dan Hughes)	(2013)	**(STL)**
Teenagers & Attachment (in Perry, Ed.)	(2009)	**(TA)**
Senior Manager in School	(2016)	**(SMiS)**
Team Pupil in School	(2016)	**(TPiS)**

Part One

Becoming a Key Adult

The aim of this book
This book supports individuals who undertake the incredibly important role of **Key Adult** with troubled children and young people. It will help **Key Adults** understand the work they will be doing with pupils in school and how they can best contribute to the team around the child or young person - Team Pupil. I will also be discussing how the **Key Adult** can advocate for the pupil within the wider school context and with allied professionals.

What does a Key Adult do – and why?
The aim of the support work is to enable the **attachment systems** of these children and young people to be attended to in the school context, so that their **exploratory systems** can be freed up. As a consequence, they will be able to make the most of their time at school, taking up the hundreds of opportunities available to them.

The Key Adult in School

In other words, by providing the pupil with a **secure attachment** or relationship (with the **Key Adult**), we enable the child or young person to feel safe enough to feel curious, to be open to learning. This happens by effectively 'taming' the child or young person into a healthy relationship with a grown-up (the **Key Adult**) in school, so that trust develops through the facilitation of over-compensatory safety, security and stability. By gently challenging the pupil's perceptions and by giving them both the space and time they need to lay aside 'ghosts' from the past and the opportunity to update how they view themselves, other people and the world, they will eventually be able to settle to learn.

> We need to feel trust to be vulnerable and we need to be vulnerable in order to trust.   Brown 2012, p.47

A **Key Adult** can be supported to spend at least 30 minutes a week out of class with a troubled pupil on a 1:1 basis. However, there are many children and young people out there in our schools who would benefit from much more regular contact and check-ins throughout the school day and week, in and out of their classes. Alongside in class: a quick check-in, in the reception area, classroom or inclusion department. Time in the Safe Space together for some downtime. Out and about round school: in a private room or space, for some 1:1 withdrawal work. Or even off-site together, for example, at an allotment project.

Strong emotional connection appears to be associated with improved outcomes and it may be that relationship closeness is more important than the amount of contact and the types of activites engaged in.

Spencer et al 2010, *quoted in* Cameron et al 2015, p.105

Some **Key Adults** support the children and young people they are working with for up to a maximum of 20 plus hours per week. The time allocated by the **Key Adult** depends on the needs of the child or young person at home and school: remembering that what is presented by their mood or behaviour is not always indicative of what is actually happening for them, in the here-and-now, or what they really need. Many children and young people who are hurting have got very good at hiding what they really yearn for: so in this work, we have to focus on their hidden needs - the ones we've recognised (through our training, background reading and our knowledge of their history) require attention and response.

In this work we will need to attend to the pupil's *expressed* needs: but most of our work will need to be focussed on their *hidden* needs. Decisions about time to be allocated will be made by you and your colleagues in Team Pupil depending on your thorough knowledge of your Key Pupil at the different phases of your journey alongside them (*and see* **TPiS** pp.34-7).

The Key Adult in School

Ideal qualities of a Key Adult

Experienced in working and relating to children with emotional and behavioural difficulties

Resilient ☆ Sense of humour ☆ Robust

Balanced approach to difficulties using both nurture and structure

Flexibility of thinking ☆ Not easily shocked

Able to work as part of a team with other education staff, other agencies and parents/carers

Positive sense of self ☆ Regulated ☆ Empathic

Able to listen to and act on advice

Imaginative ☆ Resourceful

Able to advocate for pupil within the wider school context and with allied professionals

Calm ☆ Tenacious

Available on a long-term basis in school - (not on a temporary contract or planning to leave shortly!)

Playful ☆ Accepting ☆ Curious

Knows own history, and when to ask for help or referral

(from Bombèr 2007, p.67)

Core aims of the Key Adult-Key Pupil relationship

The Key Adult's aims in creating the relationship with the pupil will be to help the child or young person to

1. develop trust in the **Key Adult**, by experiencing having her consistently emotionally and physically available

2. manage his or her feelings, by receiving sensitivity of response from the **Key Adult**, who attunes herself to her Key Pupil

3. develop an increased sense of self-esteem by experiencing acceptance

4. feel effective by being engaged in relationships with both adults and peers

(from Bombèr 2007, p.84)

The Key Adult in School

Good questions about a Key Adult

↳ *Will this mean that our classes will be packed with Key Adults - particularly in deprived areas?*

No - not all children need **Key Adults** to be actively involved with them all the time. Despite difficult situations, some children have incredible resilience and manage to do very well at school, despite the odds. This means that **Key Adults** can and do have many other responsibilities and are not necessarily resident in the pupil's classroom! **Key Adults** are needed for children who have experienced **relational trauma** and loss and who are struggling in school and/or at home in some way. What they do, and how much time is allocated, will be determined by the pupil's needs as well as their present and future risks. Time invested now will mean less expense later. It is a no-brainer (*and see* **TPiS** pp. 5-11 *on identifying which children would benefit from the Key Adult/Team Pupil approach*).

↳ *Does the Key Adult work with just one child and no-one else?*

No - the **Key Adult** can key-work other children, but let's be sensitive, and not parade this to them! For example, a **Key Adult** might key-work pupils in different year groups. A **Key Adult** in a special setting might see individual members of the group away from the prying eyes of the class! It's important that when the **Key Adult** is with her Key Pupil that she behaves as if he is the only child or young person in her care. These pupils need our full attention and sensitive care. If the Key Pupil asks about other pupils in your care, don't lie: respond firmly to questions with the fact that this is his time right now, and you don't want to be wasting his time by talking about X or Y. Emphasise that this is quality time for him.

↳ Does the *Key Adult* remain with the Key Pupil forever?

No - the amount and use of time spent with the pupil needs to be matched to his or her development. It is good practice in attachment terms to invest a lot of time and energy early on, and then to slowly reduce this level of commitment over time - in line with the pupil's growing independence, not in line with our school systems! Please do be careful to reduce *contact* very gradually though, as you will soon know if growth wasn't assessed accurately! The pupil needs to experience gradual reduction in contact as evidence of their ability to respond appropriately and healthily. Please note that in some cases this can take a few years, because of the levels of distress and damage the child or young person has experienced. Also I need to clarify that the relationship with the **Key Adult** needs to remain, even after contact has been reduced. Let's replicate real life! Relationships are meant to carry on. Together we can consider how. Some of my pupils continue to see their **Key Adults** even after they have left their school, with professional boundaries in place. Attachment needs to be honoured.

The Key Adult in School

↳ *How is this support best funded?*

I encourage schools to use existing staff differently. Firstly, to assess which staff are best matched to this kind of work, as it will be more cost effective to allocate those who have the right skills and qualities (*see* p.12). They are more likely to find the work rewarding and stay in post for longer. Permanency will thus reduce overall support costs. So most of the time, existing staff can be allocated to work with these pupils. If necessary, it is possible to top up their hours with the Pupil Premium and with additional needs funding. Schools do have budgets allocated to support vulnerable pupils and can usually approach the Virtual School in their local authority if they need a top-up.

Part Two

The Key Adult and the Team Pupil

The **Key Adult** is the person who develops the closest relationship in the school context with a particular pupil. This relationship is central to attachment aware support work in school. The **Key Adult** becomes the expert on the pupil in the school context. She or he makes it their business to be curious and to learn all about this individual pupil - their stressors and their calmers.

The **Key Adult** is then referred to by the rest of Team Pupil, so that he or she is always the first port of call in relation to the pupil. These other Team members provide the increased or decreased structure and supervision necessary within their different roles and responsibilities, as the work with the Key

The Key Adult in School

Pupil develops and evolves over time. They also advocate for the pupil in different circumstances, ensuring the pupil's needs are remembered, sometimes even representing the pupil's voice in appropriate contexts. They all know the plan and ensure consistent practices are employed (the roles and responsibilities of each of the other members of Team Pupil are unpacked further within the **Attachment Aware School Series** of pocket books for the individuals doing this work).

All other staff in the wider school community are encouraged to refer to the Team, so that it will be the Team which makes any direct or indirect intervention: for sharing strengths and vulnerabilities, for sharing successes and difficulties, for increased structure and supervision when unhealthy or inappropriate behaviours are observed, for holding boundaries, for discipline and for check-ins. This creates a *small world* for the pupil (Forbes 2011), enabling tight teamwork and consistent practice. So the pupil will experience consistency, and will feel held emotionally.

The pupil's attachment needs are best identified initially by an **Attachment Lead** in the school or authority. However, do remember that at a later stage in some cases it may be appropriate to refer to a trauma expert, as some may need a specialist intervention. Sometimes attachment aware interventions may not be enough, so the trauma specialist can collaborate in providing the Team

Attachment aware and trauma informed support for those who are hurting in schools

(drawing on the Seguridad model used by TouchBase™ © theyellowkite.co.uk)

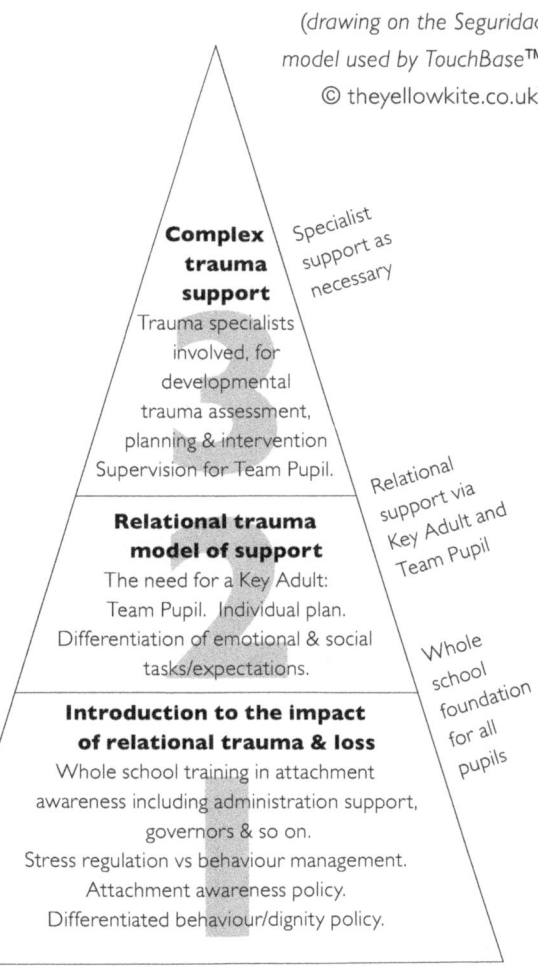

Complex trauma support
Trauma specialists involved, for developmental trauma assessment, planning & intervention Supervision for Team Pupil.

Specialist support as necessary

Relational trauma model of support
The need for a Key Adult: Team Pupil. Individual plan. Differentiation of emotional & social tasks/expectations.

Relational support via Key Adult and Team Pupil

Introduction to the impact of relational trauma & loss
Whole school training in attachment awareness including administration support, governors & so on.
Stress regulation vs behaviour management.
Attachment awareness policy.
Differentiated behaviour/dignity policy.

Whole school foundation for all pupils

The Key Adult in School

with a map through unchartered territory. What is needed and what interventions and relationships are required to support the pupil will be discussed and modified over time with Team Pupil, as the work progresses and the pupil begins to settle to learn (*see structure on previous page*).

On allocation, the Team can have a photo taken together with their Key Pupil. This is a good opportunity to explain to the pupil each person's role in supporting him or her to make the most of all the educative opportunities on offer in school. Team members can each keep a copy of the photo - as can the pupil.

They can then re-group every now and again to remind the pupil that they are rooting for him or her! We need to be very explicit. Remember they get mixed up with other people's motives and intentions - so imagine the pupil's surprise when they realise this Team is just for them, giving them evidence that adults can and do notice, attend to and respond to their needs. This immediately challenges perception.

On a Friday, a **Key Adult** will complete a Home/School Partnership prompt sheet detailing stressors and calmers observed in the past week, and any anticipated ones foreseen for the coming week (Bombèr 2007, p.272). This can be sent to the family, ideally by email. On a Sunday evening, the family can complete the same partnership prompt sheet and send it to the team for Monday morning (again, ideally by email - beware of the child having to be a carrier), so that the Team are ready for the week ahead.

Team Lee!

The Key Adult in School

Responsibilities of Key Adults

> Compassion is the basis of all morality.
> Arthur Schopenhauer

Compassion lies behind each of these responsibilities.

▷ Attending to the child - commentating, wondering aloud, providing a narrative, adjusting your relationship style to your Key Pupil
▷ Establishing a strong bond with the pupil
▷ Providing opportunities to repair ruptures in relationships together
▷ Enabling the pupil to build a robust sense of self
▷ Developing curiosity in the pupil
▷ Making connections on behalf of the pupil
▷ Becoming a fellow traveller especially when the going gets tough
▷ Providing over-compensatory nurture
▷ Facilitating creative solutions when difficulties are encountered
▷ Providing gentle challenge
▷ Lending your thinking brain when the pupil's brain is immature and/or off-line
▷ Co-modelling appropriate and healthy responses and ways of being
▷ Providing emotional holding and containment - being consistent

- Letting the pupil know he is being held in mind
- Being a stress and shame regulator
- Creating opportunities for the child or young person to practise new ways of being and doing so that these pupils grow stronger
- Communicating empathy
- Instilling hope
- Highlighting ways in which the school keeps the pupil safe by noticing them out loud
- Providing sensory integration opportunities
- Advocating for the pupil within the wider school context
- Knowing the difference between attachment aware and 'trauma informed' practice
- Recognising when to refer to more specialist trauma support
- Recognising when you need help and support
- Liaising with the other members of Team Pupil, to ensure that you receive the kind of support you need to do your job well

The Key Adult in School

Don't be alarmed - you don't have to learn this all in one sitting! And you won't be working in isolation. A lot of what I'm describing here will make sense to you over time. It will be worth re-visiting and highlighting sections in this book, and checking out the other books in the Series. I also recommend that you have your foundation books (*see* p.65) to hand as well. These books are all written in such a way that you can make quick reference to whatever might come up as you journey with your pupil.

Working with other members of Team Pupil

Remember too that you are now a part of a Team around your Key Pupil. You will have your own **Key Adult** checking in with you, your senior manager on the pupil's team. Everyone needs a **Key Adult**! It may also be that your local authority is now facilitating support groups, as advocated in the **Attachment Lead** training I deliver across the UK. If so, get plugged in! It's great to meet others in similar roles facing similar challenges. It may also be that your school already has an **Attachment Lead** in place. If so, they will have a wealth of experience and resources that they can share with you. Do make the time to link in and connect. There is great possibility in togetherness.

It is essential to work on growing positive connections with the parents/carers of the pupil you are allocated. They will be playing such a significant part in this pupil's adaption

10 things Key Adults say to encourage anyone new taking up the role:

- He used to have meltdowns that could go on for hours. Now he gets going again after about 5 or 10 minutes!

- You start to realise that support work is not a 'just' but is invaluable.

- It is such a privilege to be involved in another's life so closely!

- I didn't know much about attachment when I first started but I do now. I wish I'd known what I know now as the change in him is considerable.

- It takes time but my, what a difference now.

- I have seen him transform over time. I never thought it would be possible but wow!

- You start to do what you knew was right all along!

- You have permission to build genuine relationships.

- When I first tried to work with him I sometimes had to go and get him from class, he would hide away with hardly any eye contact. Now he is so much better! He is happy to come along, looks me right in the eye and talks.

- We learn how to be truly human.

The Key Adult in School

and recovery, as will you. Make time to link in with them whenever you can. You can use the Home/School Partnership prompt sheets weekly (*see* p.21)

And, on a more informal basis, please make sure there's space for you to smile together, laugh together, share together and journey together. Our pupils are watching. They notice everything! They are watching how we interact and are noting how we relate. Together, our consistency of approach will increase their sense of felt safety.

Part Three

So - let's get going!

Well, welcome to your new role! It's great that you've made this decision to help some of our most vulnerable children and young people. I imagine you're probably wondering what you've let yourself in for!

Let's start by developing better self-awareness, so that as a **Key Adult**, you can be in the best state you can be, and relate well. It will be important that you know what has shaped you and made you who you are today, because we are all affected by our **attachment history**.

So we'll begin by looking at how significant other people have related to us in the past and present, and explore how we've responded, what we've learned to date, and what we still have to work on. I'll be providing you with some exercises to do alone or, ideally, with someone else. We will focus especially on our parents/carers and our closest friends and family. I'll be inviting you to consider how much

The Key Adult in School

you *know your own story*, and also to think about how you *manage your stress*.

Throughout, I'll be asking you to think about how you *look for and use support*, something we all need to be good at doing in this work and in life. I'll provide you with some examples of stress plans, which you can adapt to your own situation.

The more self-aware we are, the better role models we can be. The more secure, integrated and reflective we can be emotionally, the better able we'll be to lead our pupils into developing new emotional and mental capacities themselves.

Finally, I'll look at the *specific roles* you'll be taking up as a **Key Adult**.

A KNOW YOUR OWN STORY

Have you ever wondered why you do what you do? What has made you into the person you now are? Have you ever considered the impact your own attachment history might have on you? As human beings we are experience-dependent, meaning that how we are and what we think, feel and do, are all shaped by our experiences - for better or for worse. We all know that in our work role, it's really important that we are curious about the pupil/s in our care. However, that curiosity needs to start with us. To strengthen our capacity for curiosity, we first need to be curious about ourselves, and a great place to start is by asking ourselves questions.

Before we get started, I'd like to reassure you that this journey of self-discovery is not a means of judging ourselves or each other. In fact, the opposite is true - it's about *increasing* our self-acceptance and empathy. Neither is it merely a 'navel-gazing' exercise. The more self-aware we are, the more helpful we can be when relating to those who have experienced the most extraordinary **toxic stress** (*see* **Glossary**), as many of the children and young people we come across in schools have done.

Self-awareness is the stepping stone towards 'other' awareness. Allowing yourself to be vulnerable and to open up a little can mean that as a **Key Adult**, you'll be in a position to offer troubled pupils your best qualities and capacities.

The Key Adult in School

> Vulnerability is the birthplace of love, belonging, joy, courage, empathy, and creativity. It is the source of hope, empathy, accountability, and authenticity. If we want greater clarity in our purpose or deeper and more meaningful lives, vulnerability is the path.
>
> Brown 2012, p.34

So what I'm going to be suggesting is that you enter into a *reflective dialogue* with yourself. And to help you do this, I'll provide some exercises to gently challenge you to explore who you are and why you do what you do. You may want to try reflective journaling so that you can then track back over the journey you make. Journaling can involve writing, drawing or even sticking bits and pieces into a notebook - whatever you like, really! Make it your book about you and use whatever media you feel most comfortable with.

As part of this journey of discovery about yourself I recommend that you ask someone who knows you well to get alongside you to be your travelling companion. We all need someone, if we're going to truly know ourselves and others, as it's through connection that we learn more of who we are. Accepting and empathic others can be like mirrors, revealing things to us that we may not have even noticed before, nudging us out from places where we may have got stuck, urging us on into healthier ways of being and relating.

For example, we can often underestimate or not notice parts

of ourselves that others might value and appreciate. At the same time, we are not always aware of our own 'shadows', those parts of us that are not so well developed or are even damaged, that may cause us difficulties interpersonally. Someone we trust can help highlight these without causing us to feel shamed or defensive. Choose someone you have known for a while that you trust, someone who can give constructive feedback and help begin to fill in gaps in your self-awareness.

Set aside some protected, private time to have a go at the exercises that follow. Please don't think I'm suggesting you complete all the exercises in one go! You will get more from each exercise if you complete them over several weeks, so that you can allow yourself some processing time. They are intended to be completed in the order I've given so that you can gradually become increasingly vulnerable with yourself and with the person alongside you; even with ourselves, we need to build a safe platform to be in a position to trust ourselves in this process. And your responses don't need to be shared with anyone other than your trusted other person: but of course that's up to you. You could perhaps consider arranging some regular meet-ups with your trusted person, so you can discuss what you will share and what you won't, and what you would like their comments on or help with.

If you find that you're getting distressed completing any of the exercises, press the pause button and go a little slower,

The Key Adult in School

ensuring you seek support as appropriate. It's up to you how much you disclose to yourself and to the person you're working with. I would urge you towards openness though - even if it feels a bit uncomfortable initially.

Remember you won't get in touch with more than you can handle if you allow yourself to be vulnerable: 'Whatever is shareable is bearable' (Siegel 1999). Also, it's important to be aware that we often assume we're weaker than we actually are. Many of the difficult experiences we've lived through have left us with strength which has been born out of courage. It's not a cliché to recognise that often, there are truly many treasures to be stumbled upon in the darkest times of life.

You may find that your curiosity starts to develop more whilst you are engaging with the exercises I've suggested. It doesn't have to stop here! Go on and ask yourself more questions and set yourself further exercises. Let's strengthen our curious part. It's a part that will serve us well as we get alongside troubled children and young people.

This first group of activities/exercises invites you to think about what makes you the unique person you are. You will find yourself asking questions as to why you do what you do. These exercises are helpful because they are designed to build self-awareness. The process will be fascinating!

EXERCISE 1 NAMING ME

Let's reflect on how we describe ourselves. Choose three adjectives to describe you.

REFLECTION

Think about why you chose these particular adjectives.

- How could you use this new awareness to support the troubled pupil in your care?

EXERCISE 2 THE PARTS PICTURE

Let's reflect on the different parts that make us who we are: after all, we are all a combination of parts.

Get a large piece of paper and map out all the parts that make you who you are. Start with the parts of yourself that you are happy with, or even proud of. If you love reading, for example, note your reading part. If you can paint, note your painting part. Your kind part, your patient part, your welcoming part, your thoughtful part, and so on.

That's the easy bit! Now that you have a sense of your more positive interests and qualities,

The Key Adult in School

attempt to be a little vulnerable. Start noting down those aspects of yourself that you don't like, aren't proud of and maybe are even ashamed of. Take your time. Notice how your parts connect up, complement, conceal, compete or even come into conflict with one another. For example you may have both a patient and an impatient part.

Interestingly, these parts pictures will change over time as we change, shaped by our experiences. Use arrows to indicate which parts you would like to pay more attention to, to strengthen, and which parts you would like to shrink. Again, be honest. Do ask your friend or partner to add in some of their own reflections to this process.

REFLECTION

Think about your parts picture in its entirety.

- Is this how you thought you were made up before you started this exercise? Any surprises? Anything you want to change? Maybe ask yourself how these parts might have developed.
- How could you use this new awareness to support the troubled pupil in your care?

EXERCISE 3 RELATIONSHIP CIRCLES

Let's consider who we are connected to and in what order of significance.

Get a large piece of paper and draw three large circles within each other. Write your name in the centre. In each circle, write down those you consider closest to you, working your way out from the centre to those who are more like acquaintances in the largest circle. Then think through who you might put further out than even the third circle, perhaps even in the corners of the page or over the page or those you would not want anywhere on your relationship circles.

REFLECTION
Think about what your relationship circles may be showing you.

- How easy was this exercise for you?
- How did you determine what 'closest to you' means for you?
- How connected are you? Do you have a good support network? Or are you quite isolated? Would you like more people on your inner circles?
- If so, how could you put yourself in situations where new connections might be possible?

The Key Adult in School

If you have placed individuals further out on the outer rings or in the corner or over the page, ask yourself how they influence you at this time.

- Are you comfortable with where they are or would you prefer them to be closer?
- If you would prefer more intimacy with them, what will you do to encourage this?
- If you want them to remain at a distance, think about what has formed a barrier in your connection? Has there been any kind of disruption? Is there no way back through to any kind of reunion or repair?

Think about how satisfied you are with your level of connections.

- Do you feel you have all you need?
- If not, what do you need?
- How can you work towards building further connection?

    *Remember **Key Adults** need their own **Key Adults** in order to remain healthy themselves. Interdependency promotes health and well-being. If you are going to be part of a support network for a troubled pupil it is essential that you have our own support network intact and thriving.*

- How could you use this new awareness to support the troubled pupil in your care?

EXERCISE 4 THINKING ABOUT FAMILY AND HOME

Let's dig a little deeper, exploring what we mean by the words family and home. We have all had very different experiences and our interpretations will affect how we are and what we do.

☐ Draw or write what you understand by the word **FAMILY**

☐ Draw or write what you understand by the word **HOME**

REFLECTION
Notice as you do this any states, sensations or feelings in your body. Notice what you are thinking in your mind and what you are feeling in your heart.

- What does this tell you about your experiences? How do you think your experiences affect you within your role?
- How could you use this new awareness to support the troubled pupil in your care?

The Key Adult in School

EXERCISE 5 THE LIFE GRAPH

Let's reflect on our life journey to date and plot it out on a graph so we can see the ups and the downs and notice any patterns formed.

☐ Get a large piece of paper and draw a horizontal line half way down the page. Mark the line at regular intervals from 0 to your age plus ten years. Draw a vertical line on the far end of the horizontal line. Mark the vertical line with *good* and *very good* above the horizontal line. Mark the vertical line with *bad* and *very bad* below the horizontal line.

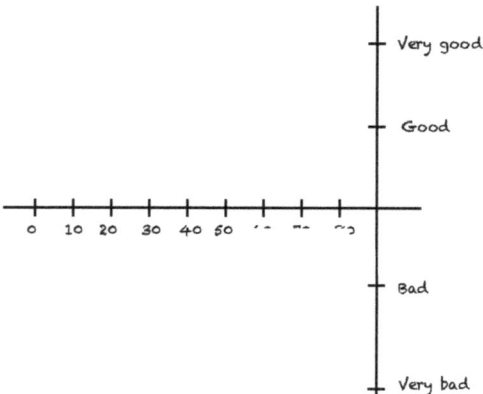

☐ Now, using or drawing stars, mark how you experienced life as a baby (0) up to your age now in red. Now, using or drawing stars, mark how you think you might experience life in the future in blue.

It is up to you if you want to write any notes on your graph. If you do, I would recommend just titles rather than writing too much detail.

☐ Now join the stars up. Think about your life journey so far and on your future. Consider what you had choices about, and what was outside your control in the past. Think about what you will have choices about and what might be outside your control in the future.

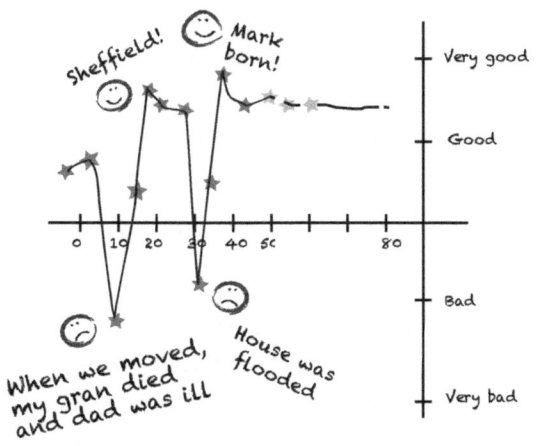

REFLECTION

Take some time to focus on your life graph.

- Do you feel this represents your journey well?
- Have you noticed any patterns?

The Key Adult in School

- If you have, what are they?
- Have you had a relatively stable life journey or have there been single or multiple incidents along the way that have caused significant disruption?
- If you have experienced disruption, have you recovered? If not, are you working towards some kind of adaption or recovery?
- If you are, how are you facilitating this?
- If not, how come? What is blocking you? What support might you need to get through this block? Where can you find that? What would be the first step?
- How could you use this new awareness to support the troubled pupil in your care?

EXERCISE 6 THINKING ABOUT MOTHER AND FATHER

Let's push ourselves a little deeper still! Let's now reflect on the primary attachment figures in our own lives: our parents.

☐ Draw or write what you understand by the word **MOTHER**

☐ Draw or write what you understand by the word **FATHER**

REFLECTION
- How come you have written or drawn what you have? What has influenced this?
- Would you have written/drawn the same as a child, adolescent or young adult? Do you think you might write/draw something different in, say, ten years' time?
- If you are a parent, grandparent or carer now yourself, how has your experience of being parented affect your parenting? And for all of us: how does our experience of being parented affect our support work?

How could you use this new awareness to support the troubled pupil in your care?

EXERCISE 7 INVENTORY

Let's get close and personal. Let's consider our value systems, which deeply affect how we see ourselves, others and the contexts we find ourselves in. They also affect why we do what we do right now.

Consider these questions and answer them as honestly as you can:

1 What would you love to do before you die?

The Key Adult in School

2. Is there anything you regret?
3. Can you think of any life event that has had a profound impact on you?
4. What are your unrealised dreams?
5. Is there any aspect of yourself that you would like to get better at?
6. Do you show others your true self?
7. Would you consider yourself a good friend?
8. Do you hide aspects of yourself?
9. Is there anyone who has positively influenced you?
10. Are you bitter about anything?
11. If someone started opening up to you, how would you respond?
12. Is there anything you feel you need to resolve?
13. What do you feel you contribute to others?
14. Do you have any blocks to building relationships?
15. How would you like others to remember you?

REFLECTION
Check back over your responses.

- How easy was that to do?
- How well did you know yourself?
- Is there anything there that has surprised you? Have you noticed any patterns?
- Is there anything you are not comfortable with?

- Is there anything that has come to mind that you would now like to do differently, as a result of working through that exercise?
- How could you use this new awareness to support the troubled pupil in your care?

EXERCISE 8 THINKING ABOUT COMFORT, DISCIPLINE AND STRESS

Let's reflect on our own experience of nurture. If we received nurture, what shape did it take? Let's reflect on how we were socialised. Did it help us or did it harm us in any way?

Let's reflect on what kinds of things stressed us as children, and how we managed stress back then and how we manage stress right now. All our experiences shape us in some way, for better or for worse.

- Consider the word **COMFORT**.
  Were you comforted as a child? How?
- Consider the word **DISCIPILINE**.
  Were you disciplined as a child? How?
- Consider the word **STRESS**.
  Were you stressed as a child? In what way?
  How did you manage this stress?
  How do you receive comfort nowadays?
  Can you ask for what you need?

The Key Adult in School

REFLECTION
Let's explore the descriptions you have written.

- Are there any surprises? Are there any patterns?
- Why do you think it might be especially important to trace back our own experiences in all of this to be able to be an effective **Key Adult**?
- How could you use this new awareness to support the troubled pupil in your care?

EXERCISE 9 BALLOONS & WEIGHTS
Let's reflect on what weighs us down and what frees us up. This will be different for everyone dependent on our experiences to date, our life stage and our home and work situation.

☐ Draw six big balloons at the top of a large piece of paper. At the bottom, draw six big heavy weights (see p.46).
☐ In the balloons, write anything that activates, uplifts or energises you: for example walking, running, watching a sunset, having a hug, drinking wine!

- ☐ In the weights, write down anything that saps energy from you, leaving you feeling drained and low: for example, doing paperwork, a long commute in the traffic, being around a particular colleague (as she demands a lot of emotional energy or makes work demands).

REFLECTION
Now think about the things you have identified and consider why you might have chosen what you did, and why you experience each of them in this way. As you reflect on your list, notice anything that that might support you to move forwards, perhaps in the direction of getting or increasing support or freedom, or whatever else you feel you need.

- What do you consider to be your personal responsibility and what do you believe is someone else's responsibility?
- How much have you mentioned people? Does this reveal anything about your attachment style?
- Does this reveal anything about your support network?
- Has there ever been a time when you could do absolutely nothing to feel more comfortable internally?
- Would there be anything you can do to make yourself feel more comfortable next time?

The Key Adult in School

EXERCISE 9 WHAT WEIGHS DOWN AND WHAT FREES US UP?

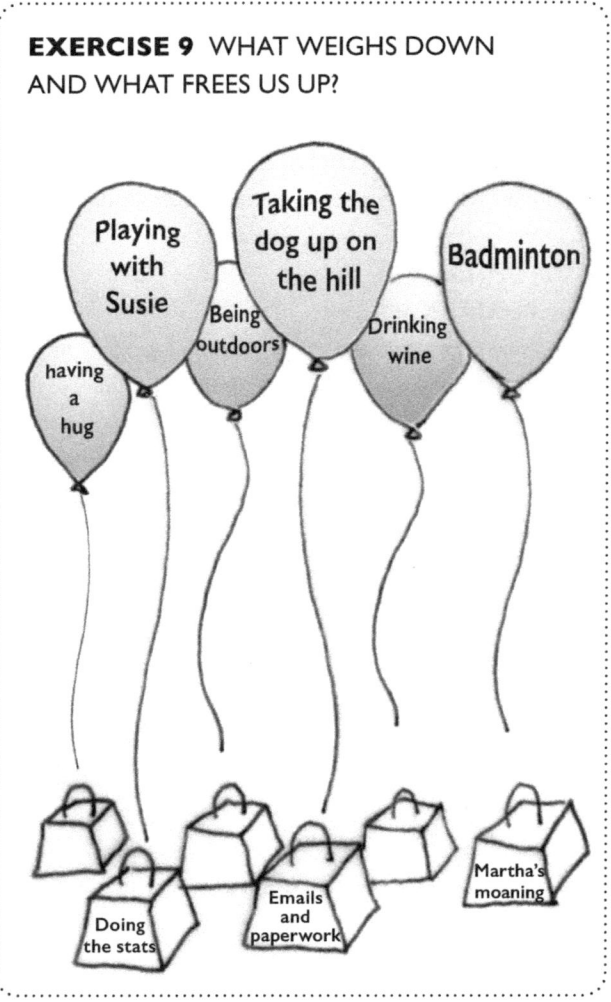

- How could you use this new awareness to support the troubled pupil in your care?

EXERCISE 10 SEMPS LEVELS

Let's reflect on how we are doing on a regular basis. Let's be mindful and notice what is going on internally as we go through our days. Try and get into a daily routine of checking in on what we can think of as our 'SEMPS levels:

S stands for Spiritual level
E for Emotional level
M for Mental level
P for Physical level
The final **S** stands for Social level.
Give yourself a number out of 10, 10 being the best score you could be!

REFLECTION

- What are the factors that help you improve your levels? What factors tend to reduce them?
- Think about what you might need to do - or not do - to move these levels up a notch or two!
- How could you use this new awareness to support the troubled pupil in your care?

The Key Adult in School

B MANAGE YOUR STRESS

Working alongside pupils who have lived through or are living with extraordinary stress in their relationships will undoubtedly evoke stress in us. So it will be important that we reflect on our own stress levels, and how we manage or don't manage stress.

Firstly, we need to think about the difference between *ordinary* life stressors and *extraordinary* stressors. Consider how much stress you have experienced and whether your 'window of stress tolerance' - (what Heather Forbes (2012) and others describe as your capacity for remaining within your usual equilibrium before tipping into a state of feeling overwhelmed) has been compromised in any way.

Life, being full of change, is stressful. In fact, any kind of transition, even getting up in the morning from our beds to move into the kitchen, activates our stress response! Our bodies and minds are designed in such a way as to manage small doses of stress on a daily basis. However, if we experience some of the more challenging stressors for a protracted period, our functioning can be severely affected.

Let's have a look at Sîan and Liza. Sian has experienced ordinary everyday stressors in her life so far. But in early childhood Liza experienced an overdose of extraordinary stress. Both Sîan and Liza have what I think of as an 'overwhelm button', when they are too full up with stress and start to flood, leading to what are known as the **fight/flight or freeze** responses (*see* p.51).

Now, when an everyday stressor occurs for Sîan, her window of tolerance is quite expansive, so she is able to cope with quite a lot before moving into overwhelm. However, because Liza's window of tolerance is smaller, because of what has happened to her already, when an everyday stressor occurs for Liza, *her* overwhelm button gets activated easily as if there were an emergency.

This means that Liza moves into fight/flight or freeze responses even if the stressor is quite minor (for example, travelling to work). In another context, Sîan might find that she feels uncomfortable on experiencing a slight stressor, but Liza presents an over-reactive response, screaming and swearing.

So, in light of this information, try exploring your own experience and responses:

- List the stressors around for you when you were a child
- Identify which of these were *ordinary stressors*, and which were *extraordinary stressors*.
- List the stressors around for you now as an adult
- Identify which of these are ordinary stressors and

The Key Adult in School

which are extraordinary stressors
- How do you feel you manage stress?
- How would you know you were stressed?
- How would others know you were stressed?
- How do you experience your *zone of tolerance*?
- When does your *overwhelm button* go off?
- What do you do, or what can others do, to calm or soothe you?
- Create a Stressometer from 1 to 10, 1 being when you are most relaxed, 10 being when you feel overwhelmed.

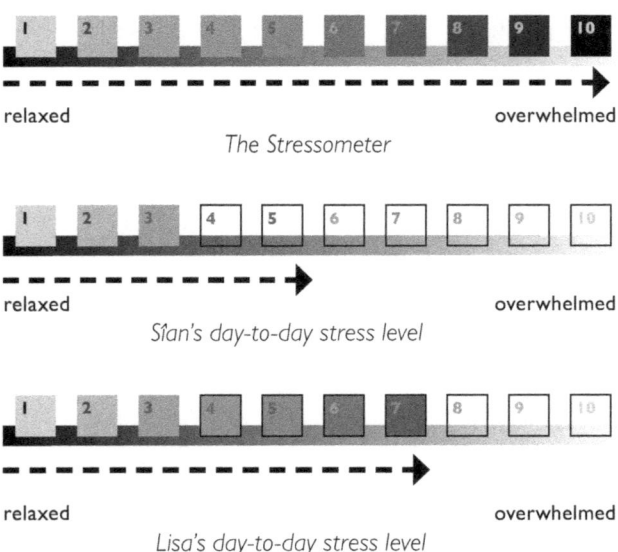

The Stressometer

Sían's day-to-day stress level

Lisa's day-to-day stress level

During this next week, use your stressometer every day to measure your stress levels. Notice what stresses you out most, and what relaxes or soothes you most. All of us tend to use one of three defence mechanisms (or a combination) when we feel stressed.

FIGHT	becoming argumentative, feisty, aggressive, swearing, being critical and judgmental, getting controlling
FLIGHT	hiding behind someone, leaving, sweeping things under the carpet, changing the subject, walking out, avoiding a truth or a person, acting helpless
FREEZE	daydreaming, shutting things out, 'forgetting', lying low, sleeping, eating or drinking lots, procrastinating, losing sense of ourselves, even losing feeling for our bodily functions

Work out which is your most typical response to stress. It will probably be one that served you well in the past or it may be an adaptive one, one you developed when an earlier strategy you'd developed didn't serve you so well.

The Key Adult in School

As human beings, we tend to clearly remember when and how we were hurt, distressed, traumatised or abused (and sadly, without conscious effort, we don't tend to remember all the good stuff nearly as clearly!). This is because we have in-built defence mechanisms to help us to stay safe and well, to overcome adversity, to survive; perhaps remembering difficult times and how we coped (or didn't cope) is part of this process.

However, when you have experienced extraordinary stress, your alarms can go off even when they don't need to. If this is the case, then it's likely that your alarm system has become faulty, due to having been activated so much previously. Others are likely to notice your over-reactions to minor stressors, and may wonder what has happened to you to make you so tense and reactive.

Now to the brave ask with this aspect of self-awareness. Ask the person who you're working with whether they have ever noticed this in you. Please don't be overly concerned if you find you do have a somewhat 'faulty' alarm system, as you can 'tame' it and re-train it to go off when it actually needs to go off - rather than every time there is a low level, ordinary, everyday stressor. Now that it is in your awareness, anything is possible!

If you do think your alarm system is faulty at the moment, try and think about how this could have happened, how it might be linked to stressors in your past. Remember to be kind to yourself. Many of us are more self-critical than nurturing.

Remember that if your alarm is faulty it is probably as a result of **toxic stress**. Usually, toxic stress is caused by external sources. In many ways, this idea isn't complicated. If you have had too much stress in your life to date, you will need to do everything you can to ensure you are nurtured or comforted lots now. As adults, we need to take responsibility to ensure we are topped up with nurture and comfort. Of course even adults sometimes think this is others' responsibility, especially when they - or we - have been badly hurt or wounded. However, each one of us can choose to put ourselves in situations that bring us more nurture and comfort if that's what we notice we're lacking.

As Carolyn Spring, director of PODS (2015) advocates in her training presentations, we need to tend and care for our own 'gardens' before assisting others with theirs! We also need to remember to focus on *our* gardens and not try to take over someone else's, however much we're tempted. Our work is to empower others to get on and care for their own gardens themselves.

I find this metaphor really helpful in terms of reminding us to hold our boundaries in this work around those with overgrown, neglected, abused and sparse gardens. It's so important that we do this in a healthy way. There are many

The Key Adult in School

adults out there self-medicating, often unaware of what they are doing. Unfortunately, they are attempting to self-soothe in ways which can actually exacerbate stress levels (alcohol, drugs, gambling, food, unhealthy sex, self-harm and so on), unsettling them further. As we all know, some of these choices can actually lead to serious addictions and disease that can affect ordinary functioning; so be wise in what you choose.

Many of us have stress triggers, the kinds of things that tip us out of our usual equilibrium. Once you know what they are, you are more likely to be in a position to tame their influence on you, and look for healthy ways to self-soothe and support. But until you know what they are, they remain like time-bombs, set to go off when you least expect. Self-awareness is the necessary stepping stone to self-control. So, let's have a look at the following reflective questions:

- What makes you 'lose it'?
- What might this be linked to in your past?
- What happens to your body?
- What happens to your mind?
- What happens to your emotions?
- What do you think you are thinking/believing at that moment?
- Is this an accurate thought or belief, or are you being haunted by the past?

Next time you feel yourself 'losing it', focus on your breath and breathe your way through whatever your body, mind and emotions are communicating. Set yourself a challenge! See how long you can simply breathe for, before reacting to your alarm system. Remember your alarm system may be faulty but it's doing its best to protect you; so you may need to build in some additional processing time in order to assess the situation in hand. If you have often experienced extraordinary stress, you may not always have the filters necessary to work out how to do this, so you may need to seek advice, wisdom and support externally from someone you trust to help do so.

Many of us merely *react* to stress rather than building up our reserves to *manage* stress. Invest some time in completing the stress plan below for yourself, so that you can be preventative. Your role as a **Key Adult** (*see* Introduction) will undoubtedly be stressful from time to time, so don't be blown off course. Take action now to prepare yourself for this. Be careful, as this kind of work can be tiring, and you may slip into self-medicating almost without noticing; and remember that having your stress plan to hand is really important. You might find it helpful to laminate it, and use it daily.

> Caring for children/young people who have experienced trauma, abuse, violence or neglect is difficult work that requires physical, mental and emotional labour, a deep emotional pool on which to draw, and adequate support from a trusted other. Taylor 2011, p.11

The Key Adult in School

STRESS PLAN (1)

PREVENTATIVE PLAN OUTSIDE WORK

● PROTECTING REST TIME:

Write down how you plan to do this. Time to rest and recuperate is essential.

For example - when I get home after work, I will protect the first hour for 'me time'. I could go for a walk, a run or just chill out with a book and a cuppa

● MAINTAINING HOBBIES/INTERESTS:

Write down your hobbies and interests and alongside each one state how you plan to embrace these.

For example, guitar - I will attend a 7.30pm class every Monday. I will…

● TAKING EXERCISE:

We all know that it is healthy for us to exercise regularly, even if it's getting off a busstop earlier to walk to work. Let's think up some type of exercise that we feel comfortable doing and let's keep it up!

For example, I will go to Pilates on a Saturday morning, I'll Zumba on a Wednesday night, I'll run on a Sunday morning and Thursday evening. I will…

● THINKING ABOUT DIET:

Whilst there is so much known now about the need for a healthy balanced diet with plenty of water, fruit and vegetables, how quickly this can be exchanged for over-indulgence in sweet/salty snacks, fried foods and alcohol. So we need a new plan.

For example, when I'm at work I'll munch on apples and carrots and carry a water bottle with me. When I get in from work, I'll snack on humous and raw vegetables. I will…

● STAYING CONNECTED:

It is really important to stay connected with your family and friends. How will you do this? Yes, messaging, calling, skyping and emailing are all helpful at times, but it doesn't really replace the experience of human face-to-face contact. Write down how you plan to ensure you have that quality time with others.

For example, I will have a protected date night with my husband each week. I will see at least one of my closest girlfriends every week. I will …

The Key Adult in School

- **EXPRESSING YOURSELF:**

Who you are and what you feel is important. How will you express yourself as you go along? What is the best form of communication for you? For some it will be journaling, for others it will be chatting, or through art, or through music ...whatever your way, please protect time for this.

For example, I will write in my journal each day, even if it is just a couple of paragraphs. I will...

- **KNOWING YOUR OWN STORY:**

What is your story so far? Would you be able to write a biography of how you came to be the person you are now? Some people might want to reflect on what this might contain. Others might want to actually give it a go. Dan Hughes (2013) has written a very good book for adults to reflect on who they are and how they relate, based on attachment principles (*8 Keys to Building Your Best Relationships*). Maybe give it a go.

STRESS PLAN (2)

PREVENTATIVE PLAN AT WORK

● STRESS TRIGGERS AT WORK:

Write out anything that stresses you at work, in bullet points. Don't elaborate, or you may get more stressed! Just reminders are sufficient. When we are aware we can be more mindful. When we are more mindful, we are more able to tolerate stress and think up ways of managing it.

For example, having work dumped on me without any sense of how the extra load affects me, noise when I'm trying to concentrate, when another member of staff undermines me in front of a pupil.

● STRESS PRESENTATION AT WORK:

Write down how you know you are stressed.

For example, fast, shallow breathing; sweaty palms; not being able to think clearly; talking fast; being overly-compliant …

It may be that no-one would know apart from you, but writing it down will increase self-awareness and help you think of strategies to cope better (the next step), both of which can only be beneficial when supporting troubled pupils.

The Key Adult in School

- **STRESS RELIEVERS:**

Write down what soothes or comforts you. Try and think up healthy ones.

For example, getting some fresh air, seeing the sea, taking a hot bubble bath, phoning a close friend, playing five-a-side, even drinking a mug of custard (yes, that really is one I've come across!).

- **KEY ADULT:**

Everyone needs a **Key Adult** - not just the pupils in our care! So who are you going to choose as yours? A few of us are very privileged to have a clinical supervisor whom we feel accepted by and can trust. We need to choose someone who we trust, and who is more experienced than us, someone we respect and consider to be a good role model. I don't think it is always necessary to formally identify them as your Key Adult but it is definitely always good to have one identified in your mind.

For example, it might be your SENCO/INCO.

- **TAKING ALLOCATED BREAKS:**

However needy your assigned pupil, there will never be a case for you not having adequate breaks at work. We all need breaks in order to function well. If pressure is put on you to miss out on breaks regularly or frequently, do talk to your line manager to boundary this entitlement. If the pressure remains, contact your union rep. There are times when we need to hold our boundaries, and this is an important one. It may be that breaks need to be staggered in order for the pupil to be supported.

● END OF DAY RITUAL:
Before you leave for home, is there anything you could do in order to leave your work behind at school?

For example, talk with a colleague about your day, wash your hands slowly with some special handwash, write in a notebook, draw a picture ...

Try not to 'take your pupils home with you'. It is sometimes helpful to remember that schools are not part of the emergency services, that there will always be troubled pupils and that you only have to do your best each day when you are in school. This is not to underplay the pupils' value or to minimise their emotional and physical impact on you, but just to support you to hold your boundaries. Healthy boundaries actually support those with difficulties even if they push against them. Healthy boundaries support growth and well-being in ourselves and others.

The Key Adult in School

CRISIS PLAN AT WORK

● TAKE TIME OUT:

If there was a crisis with your pupil, how would you take time out in order to retain your reflective functioning? What would help you?

For example, would it be some solitude away from everyone in the toilets, or in the fresh air outside, or would it be connection in the staffroom? Would it be actual physical time out, for example going somewhere quite away from the pupil, or mental time out, for example doing something else like some filing or daydreaming? Everyone is different, but we can work out what works individually for us.

● SWAP INS:

If necessary, who could you swap with in order to provide some 'space' between you and your pupil? It is often helpful to pair up with someone who is maybe in the next classroom or just down the corridor, as in a crisis you are not going to be have lots of time to ask for help.

● EXPRESSING YOURSELF:

When there is a crisis, it is going to be even more important to express yourself.

Remember you may need some time before you can put into words how you are feeling. Don't make any big statements or big decisions when unsettled. When any of us experience extraordinary stress, our reflective function is compromised for a period of time. Be aware of your time lapse (time before your thinking is restored) so that you can be wise in the midst of crisis. If you are one of those who is always cool as a cucumber, then do reflect upon where your stress might be going. It has to go somewhere! For example, is it coming out through your immune system through frequent colds, allergies, aches, pains or eczema? The more we express ourselves as we go along, the less our bodies will need to complain.

● INTENSIVE CARE:

There may be odd times in your career when you cannot continue in your current role, either temporarily or, rarely, permanently. This decision must be made in the cool light of day, when your reflective functioning is back. There are times when staff need a break from this kind of work and sometimes even need to be signed off. Do value yourself and your well-being: you really matter.

The Key Adult in School

10 pieces of advice from experienced Key Adults

Get connected in. You are not alone!

Remember that what comes your way is not intended for you but for someone else from a different time, from a different place and context.

Relationships take time to build, so persevere!

Don't ever put yourself down. You have such an important role. Value it and others will learn to.

Remember these pupils have a distorted lens. Our job is to translate and translate and translate.

Don't take yourself too seriously!
Some humour goes a long way!

If you don't feel you are getting enough support keep shouting til you do!

It is important that everyone takes responsibility.
It takes a village to raise a child.

A lot of the time you have to think outside of the box. Surprise their brains!

Remember the attitude of PACE - you'll really notice the difference.

C KNOW YOUR ROLE

As a **Key Adult**, it is really important that you are very clear about what your role is going to be with the pupil in your care (*see* the list outlined earlier on p.22). As part of **Key Adult** training, my books *Inside I'm Hurting* (2007), *What About Me?* (2011) and *Settling to Learn* (2013, co-written with Dan Hughes) comprehensively map out the essential guidelines as to what a Key Adult is and how he or she can fulfil the role. I will refer to them in the text below as **IIH**, **WAM** and **STL** (*you may also find Golding et al 2013 useful*).

Here's a summary of the foundation blocks needed for building up this support work.

Safety first

The first building block is establishing safety, 'felt safety'. Creating a *'small world'* (Forbes 2011) supports these children and young people to feel safer. In the first instance, this can mean literally creating a smaller space for the pupil to have some downtime in a safe place specifically created for the purpose. This could be a tent, a room, a screened-off corner of the library: it could be a shed in a field or on an allotment! Creating a 'smaller world' can also mean reducing the number of transitions the child or young person has to go through (*see* **WAM**, 2011). We know that every transition activates the stress system and this can leave these pupils experiencing threat.

The Key Adult in School

Seat your pupil towards the back of the classroom, to the side, so they can view all that's going on and a possible exit. Being alongside a wall can be quite helpful. Increase your physical proximity as they need to know you are 'watching their back'.

If you notice scanning going on, join in, but out loud. Commentate on what is in place to help the pupil feel secure. *'Isn't it good that……'* Spotting anything that means safety will also be important. Noticing out loud is an important technique that can help with this (*see* **STL**, 2013).

Know your individual Key Pupil's stressors and do all you can to reduce their frequency and intensity at the beginning of the work. Take down/reduce the challenge and increase nurture when attempting to facilitate a felt sense of safety. We have a responsibility to be aware of the pupil's states continuum so that we can ensure all our interventions are state dependent (*see below*, drawn from Bruce Perry's state continuum, 2003).

If the pupil is starting to shift further into overwhelm then we need to intervene to bring them back into a lower state of alarm, or better still, to a calm or an alert state. Increasing sensory comfort can also really support these pupils to 'feel safe'. Consider lighting, textures, smells, atmospheres and so on.

Cognitive state	Abstract	Concrete	Emotional	Reactive	Reflexive
Internal state	Calm	Alert	Alarm	Fear	Terror

From Perry, 2003

Emotional regulation

You are there essentially to be your Key Pupil's fellow traveller, to support them to navigate the school system so that they can be all they were intended to be first time round, before their experiences of **relational trauma** (*see* **Glossary**). You are there because this pupil is not interpreting themselves, others or their contexts in a way that supports them. They look at the world through the 'lens' of **insecure attachment** developed in a situation of emotional instabilty and threat (*see* **IIH** 2007). Though this lens was 'designed' to help our pupils survive at the time when there was threat, right now their approach compromises their well-being, their functioning and their capacities.

At the moment their sense of self is quite fragile. You are going to be alongside to over-compensate for this for a while, in order to give them some protected time to get stronger and more robust in themselves. Their capacity to be open to learning will naturally unfold as a result.

The Key Adult in School

We know that these pupils will have experienced **toxic stress**, and so the way their **regulatory systems** have developed and are operating at present is compromised. This is not something they can change on their own simply through will-power. Your presence will mean that you can provide the *external* regulation that they need before they are in a position to use their own *internal* regulation.

Everyone needs external regulation through another human being in order to develop the internal regulation required to be fully human. Children and young people who've grown up in emotionally secure environments can adapt by using healthy external regulators - they understand that school staff are there to help them, even when they are strict and unsmiling. The pupils you will be working with don't have this perspective at all. They see such behaviour as threatening, and humiliating. When we are alongside our pupils, we want to optimise any and every opportunity to build their internal regulator. So you will be a *stress regulator* in your work with a child or young person, rather than a *behaviour manager*.

Individuals who never had the opportunity to experience a secure relationship as children often speak of their regret about this: they often wish they had been supported to deal with stress in healthy ways when they were much younger, rather than feeling uncontained and 'acting out' their distress These adults have to work quite hard at becoming aware of the things we've been talking about, and may for example, find practising mindfulness helpful, in itself a discipline that needs to be learned and developed, in order to quieten their minds. Spending some time in counselling or therapy is another option.

Providing connection through relationship - a human bridge

Please remember that you are not alongside this pupil to attempt to be a teacher. You are a **Key Adult** - a human bridge between **insecure attachment** and **secure attachment**, facilitating appropriate and healthy interactions so that your Key Pupil can start storing up experiences that will further their development, enabling them to thrive. With this in mind, you may sometimes find yourself alongside your pupil, together with other another staff member, as you may be needed to provide **relational buffering** for them (*see* **Glossary**), until these pupils are ready to go it alone.

I want to encourage you to get close to your pupil physically and emotionally, whatever their age. This will mean facilitating what is known as the **intersubjective experience** (*see* **Glossary**), as you both share who you are with each other.

It's possible that some people who see you with the child or adolescent you are working with may misunderstand the special relationship you are developing with your pupil, thinking you are mollycoddling them or encouraging some kind of unhealthy dependency. However, what they may not realise (and what we may have to explain) is that in order to relate in a healthy way, an interdependent way, we first need to have experienced healthy *relative dependency*. The earlier any of us experience this the better, but remember, it is never too late! It just gets trickier to develop these kinds of relationships when we're older.

You may think that 'attachment aware support' is quite counter-cultural in the school context. But if we wait until these same pupils are all grown up out there in a societal or employment context, with social and emotional difficulties, it will becomes increasingly counter-cultural. It's possible to support vulnerable adults to learn security and to learn appropriate emotional and social skills, but it takes very special people to advocate for vulnerable adults. In our society right now we tend to prefer to lock people up or hide them away as they challenge our sense of ordinary or the norm.

With their early interventions, **Key Adults** can prevent this tragic trajectory, and provide children and young people who have had the worst of starts in life with the second chance they so need and so deserve.

Providing nurture

It's important that you do all you can to fill your pupil up with nurturing experiences. Be present physically and emotionally. Be attentive. Be attuned and be responsive.

He or she really needs to experience warmth and care from you, so use any opportunity you can to top them up!

Eating and drinking together is always a helpful way to express this in a powerful way. Spending quality time together, playing and talking, smiling and laughing, is also so important for these particular children and young people. Many will have had low-level nurture, and low levels of nurture in their tanks.

The more we can attend to them the more attentive they will be. How can you give nurture away if you haven't experienced it yourself? Time spent nurturing your pupil will be another good emotional investment to enable him or her to be more emotionally and socially appropriate in the wider school context. For more detailed information on providing nurture experiences and different contexts you can create for this, please do refer to the Nurture Group Network and Theraplay® UK (*see* p.99).

The Key Adult in School

D KNOW YOUR PUPIL - AND BRING YOURSELF TO THE RELATIONSHIP

Aim to bring most of who you are into your relationship with the pupil, by which I mean sharing joint interests, challenges, joys ... whilst of course remembering that your assigned pupils are children and young people in your care, so they don't need any additional burdens of caring for you!

But we do need to bring our authenticity to the relationship. As everyone is different, this is going to mean different things for each person. Some people will reveal who they are through the outdoors, through walking, through nature, through gardening. Others will reveal who they are through the arts and literature. Others will reveal who they are through problem solving, building and solving puzzles. I could go on! What will reveal you?

Each of us has our own language of communication. The pupils are the same. Find out what their language of communication is. This will take a while with some, as their real self has had to go into hiding because of their experiences of **toxic stress**. In order to protect their fragile or **wounded selves** (Taransaud, 2011) (*see* **Glossary**) they may use an omnipotent 'mask', or a form of defence which isn't actually a true reflection of who they are. These masks are intended to keep us at a distance, so that intimacy is prevented. However, I don't want you to give up. Keep going, keep trying to find a way in. You will, but it may take some time. Time is always needed to build trust.

Smile lots and ensure you have open and positive body language. These pupils are more likely to warm to you if you can be straightforward but playful. In fact I would strongly advocate the attitude of PACE (as created and developed by Dan Hughes, 2009) in all of this support work. Here's a brief overview of the key points we find helpful in schools.

P for *playfulness*. Give yourself permission to smile, to laugh and to play - whatever the age of your pupil! We do not play enough. The best way to cement a relationship is to play together. Have fun. The more shared joy experiences we can cultivate, the better.

A for communicating *acceptance*. Show the pupil that you 'get' what they are attempting to communicate especially through their behaviour. You may not necessarily agree with the behaviour but our first step is to build a platform whereby our pupils feel 'heard'. If they don't, they are likely to shift their behaviour up another level to attempt to get your attention in a last desperate

The Key Adult in School

attempt to feel understood. In all my support groups for education staff I always say, "*Stay with the uncomfortable feelings for longer than feels comfortable,*" even if that's only two minutes more. Active listening is more powerful than you may ever realise.

C for developing *curiosity*. See yourself as a bit of a detective. Watch, wait and wonder (Muir & Lojkasek 1999). Notice out loud. Wonder out loud. This will feel odd to begin with, but you will become a natural after a while. We commentate frequently with babies and toddlers, but stop noticing and wondering as they get older. Why do we stop? It is such a helpful strategy. It builds value, worth and self-awareness. I have heard countless examples now of **Key Adults** telling me that their pupils respond to such comments with an open expression, and can sometimes even seem bewildered that you are attempting to make sense of who they are.

E is for communicating *empathy*. At any and every opportunity top them up with empathy. The more you give out, the more they receive, the more they are likely to pass on. It's a win/win!

You can read about how to extend these four attitudes within your support role, in Golding et al (2013) or you can attend a PACE or DDP Level 1 course. There are many courses widely available nowadays across the UK. Check out the DDP UK website for further information at ddpnetwork.org/uk.

I also recommend Theraplay® as a way of connecting for both the primary and secondary phases in school. Theraplay® has four dimensions: *structure, nurture, engagement* and *challenge*. All schools now need Theraplay® practitioners. For some reason schools in the UK have got left behind, but many are now realising the need for this transformative tool. You can find out more by attending Level 1 Theraplay®. Check out the Theraplay® website for further details of where and when at theraplay.org.

Gently challenging perceptions

Having often been around adults who have misused their power, authority and control, manipulating and grooming them - our pupils are going to be wary of any whiff of anything similar. They are so easily triggered. Let's surprise their brains. Remember what I wrote about in the stress section. Their alarm systems are faulty, and can go off at the slightest stressor. So research your pupil. Go search out the story, not just from the files and from meeting with those inside and outside your school who know or knew him, but watch, wait and wonder too. The most accurate story of

The Key Adult in School

what this pupil has lived through will often be played out in their behaviour. Their body, heart and mind carry the story and the evidence (Van de Kolk, 2014).

Commentate on what you see, not in a shaming way, but in a way that communicates acceptance. Wonder aloud about what you experience together with your pupil. Guess what might be going on and allow them to correct you or agree with you. Be open to learning. When you start making sense of them and what's happening for them, have a go at making connections and creating stories to support them develop a coherence of who they are, what they do and what they're like.

Your pupil will share more with you through both inappropriate and appropriate actions and words when they feel safe and settled in. Show them relentless care, even when they attempt to push you away. Be consistent and keep those promises. Show them that you are reliable and trustworthy.

There may be times when you feel a bit out of your depth. It is at these times that you do need to refer to a trauma specialist, rather than just continuing on. It is always better to err on the side of caution.

Working with Team Pupil ...

It is important in this support role that you do not work in isolation. Do connect in with the other members of Team Pupil on a regular basis. Ensure that your home/school partnership prompt sheet is copied in to the rest of the team so everyone is in the loop.

Remember that through your attentiveness, attunement and responsiveness, you will have become the expert on the pupil, so ensure your voice is heard. There will be many opportunities for you to express your views. I hear so many support staff putting themselves down because of an intergenerational culture of hierarchy that has unfortunately stuck around. Each person in the school community has value and brings something different to contribute. Why should you put yourself down? Ensure you hold your head up high. Respect your role and responsibilities and you will be surprised at how many more around you start to do the same. Be confident in the role you have and others will trust your judgment.

I know of one **Key Adult** - Geddy Naughton - who has made such a mark for herself by taking this advice seriously that you might mistake her for a member of senior management nowadays. My respect goes to **Key Adults** like Geddy, who have enabled their contribution to really matter. Your confidence will put others at ease. It will contain the anxiety that inevitably will arise from time to time in the wider

The Key Adult in School

system. Others in the team need to know you can be trusted with the task in hand. I often encourage **Key Adults** to state *"You can trust me. I know what I'm doing."*

At the same time, as I've stressed back in the Introduction, it's important to recognise the limits of our own competence, whether that's through inexperience or overwhelm. Your Senior Manager is there to be consulted, and it's important that you are honest with yourself and with her or him when you are getting out of your depth in working with the child or adolescent, if the situation is getting too challenging, or if you are simply finding it too much. The child matters - and so do you. Knowing when to ask for support is a critical ability in a **Key Adult's** repertoire of skills.

Ideally, in future, all schools will also have staff recruited and trained as Attachment Leads - please visit attachmentleadnetwork.net for more information.

If you ever hear that emails or meetings concerning your pupil are being exchanged or are going ahead without you included, please ensure you show surprise! You need to be on the circulation list and you need to be involved, as you play a key role in the life of this pupil at school.

... and with parents and carers

I know of many **Key Adults** who have made genuine connection with parents and carers, and some who have even gone on to continue meeting up after the pupils have moved onto their next educational phase. The pupil needs to see us as part of a wider team. People who really care, in fact those who engage in relentless care, no matter what. The parents and carers are obviously their primary attachment figures, and we are their additional attachment figures in school. Everything we do should complement one another, for the benefit of the child or young person.

The Key Adult in School

E ADVOCACY - WHEN THINGS GO WRONG

Sometimes things will go wrong: for example, your Key Pupil has had a stand-off with their history teacher, has punched Jimmy in the face, is absconding in the toilets, trashing the classroom ... not everyone - peers or staff - is going to see eye to eye with the pupil in your care. You will need to provide mediation from time to time, as clashes will occur when your pupil gets 'lost in translation' (**IIH**, Bombèr 2009). It is your job to provide the translation needed for either the pupil, or the other pupil or adult, or both. Often interactions can quickly move into crisis level.

Whenever possible, press the pause button and try to create some emotional and physical space for the pupil together with you alone, so that time can be built in for some processing. *Remember that often heightened stress levels will need to be attended to first, before any cognitive tasks can be employed.* It is really important that the pupil has access to the appropriate part of his or her brain in order to facilitate effective and meaningful thinking through, and reparation.

We all need to be quietened in order to think clearly. We need to be in the right emotional and physical state in order to access our higher level functioning, our thinking brain.

Some members of staff may not understand why you are engaging the pupil in something as trivial as Jenga, hanging on monkey bars or trying to pass a feather on a cushion to each other! Be prepared for odd looks or comments at first. You may need to say something as explicit as, *"Please could we book in some time together later?"* to explain some of the neuroscience or get together with the pupil's Team to determine how you are going to raise staff understanding to support your work, of Regulating, and Relating, before Reason (the 3 Rs, Perry 2014).

This will be looked at in more detail in another book in the **Attachment Aware School Series** for the Senior Managers (**SMiS**). Unfortunately, not all staff are aware of child development, attachment or neuroscience yet. I have every hope that they will be one day, when teacher training requires this knowledge. Do check out the work being carried out in this area by the Consortium for Emotional Wellbeing in Schools (*see* p.99).

When you sense (and yes, I'm trusting your judgment on this) that the pupil is ready to engage in processing whatever has got difficult, then try and sit or stand alongside him or her, rather than sitting or standing directly opposite. Try and use the word *"Let's"* as much as possible, to support the pupil to know that you remain connected and will be alongside supporting them every step of the way to repair whatever has gone wrong.

The Key Adult in School

It can really help to use pictures. If you are not an artist, blobs or stick people will do. In fact, Pip Wilson has published a number of resources using blobs (*see* **References**) that you might find helpful. Be creative, as you don't need to use a 2D picture. You could use everyday objects or nature to work things out together, or maybe a story, song or track of music. I used to work with one boy who used to use singing to process what was going on. I could feel quite self-conscious behind my therapy door wondering what my colleagues would think if they walked by hearing me singing back to him. You have to lose your inhibitions in this work!

Quite often in schools we expect pupils to work out repair plans for themselves. *"Go on, you know what you need to do! Make the right choice,"* we say. Some of our children and young people try to say the right thing, despite not 'feeling it'. I don't know about you, but I find this quite pointless. I'd rather view every difficulty as an educative opportunity. I love the way Daniel Siegel in *No Drama Discipline* (2014) talks about the need to reclaim the word 'discipline' along with its original meaning, as it means to teach. He encourages us to first *connect.* and then *redirect* by a) asking ourselves why the child or young person is acting the way they are, b) reflecting on what lesson we want to teach, and c) considering how best to teach it (2015). He also encourages us to wait until the child or young person is ready for this kind of conversation, so that they are emotionally and physically regulated. We also need to be calm and regulated ourselves. And we need to be consistent, but not rigid. Relationship and empathy first.

> Punishment might shut down behaviour in the short term, but teaching offers skills that last a lifetime.
> Siegel & Bryson 2014, p.xiv

In my work, I have found it much more effective to work things out together with the pupil, to say something like, "*We have a problem to solve today, you and me, this is what has happened and you and me are going to have a go at figuring out what we can do to put things right.*" I have noticed that as soon as I use attachment friendly words such as 'we' and 'together', these pupils seem to let down some of their sturdy defences and start to relax. They don't relax completely of course, but over time this capacity strengthens along with their growing trust.

Advocacy can be exhausting. It's hard work. I know this from the inside, as I seem to be involved in advocacy day in day out! However, that one conversation over there and that other conversation later can sometimes reap more benefits that you ever imagined. I urge you to stick in there, though it is hard. It will be worth it, and remember that even if your work is still misunderstood it won't ever be by your pupil, who notices everything! Believe me, they really do have eyes in the back of their heads. They are always watching to try and work out what we are up to.

The Key Adult in School

You may be one of those special adults they refer to one day when they are adults themselves as *"the one person who believed in me"*, *"the one person who rooted for me"*, *"the one person who understood/got me"*. What better reward for all your efforts could there be?

....

10 things that members of Team Pupil say about Key Adults, including comments from children and young people

He is really funny. He makes me laugh.
Carl, 11

He helps me a lot.
Hamid, 6

My **Key Adult** was so great; I always knew I could talk to her whatever happened.
Millie, 14

I used to be really difficult but I quite like school now. I think it's Miss Myzor. She's really nice.
Stan, 13

I wouldn't have got the grades I did without Ms Shields.
Liza, 16

Finally ...

We all have a long journey ahead. Please don't expect your work with your key pupil to be a sprint, but a marathon, so you'll need to pace yourself. With this in mind, it's important that you meet regularly with Team Pupil in school, that you stay connected with your **Attachment Lead** in school (*if there is one trained up - and see the Attachment Lead Network site (see p.99*) and with others in the local authority - maybe through support groups facilitated on a local level.

....

> I didn't want to come to school but Mr Lee used to say that he would be looking out for me. I didn't want to let him down as he is a nice guy.
> *Ryan, 13*

> The **Key Adults** have challenged others' perceptions of these children.
> *SENCO*

> Mr Sparks gets me!
> *Arjan, 15*

> The **Key Adults** in our school keep the rest of us abreast with the latest thinking in attachment, which actually helps with how we work with all our pupils.
> *Headteacher*

> I gave her a lot of grief but I know she believed in me.
> *Martin, 16*

The Key Adult in School

We all need to continue reading around this subject, so to keep abreast of the latest recommendations, have a look at the references at the end of this book. Do also read the other books in the **Attachment Aware School Series**, to find out about the work of the different members of your Team Pupil (there's one for each person) so you will be even clearer about where the boundaries of your role and responsibilities lie. It is also really helpful to follow trauma experts online, as there are many talks that are now recorded that you can watch in your own time, often at no extra expense, for example through Ted Talks and so on, on YouTube.

Let's be the best we can be. After all, these children and young people were not born into this world choosing **relational trauma** and loss. They merely did all they could to adapt and survive. Our job surely now is to ensure that their current, necessary, but temporary states of insecurity do not become life-long traits (Maté 2013).

It will be the quality relationship that you provide as **Key Adult** that will be essential to enable your Key Pupil to make this shift.

> Experiences such as therapy, mentoring, better parenting, and more benign neighbourhoods and workplaces can lead to more empathy, trust and compassion for both self and others.
>
> Music 2014

Glossary

Additional attachment figure This is the person selected in school to get alongside a child with attachment difficulties, here described as the **Key Adult**. This person could be a teaching/learning assistant or teacher, or mentor. The task is to relate to the child using strategies derived from attachment and developmental principles. Their aim is to create a relationship which will facilitate opportunities for second chance learning, so that the child can have the experience of making healthier attachments than previously. These experiences encourage the development of neural connections in the brain, which in turn leads to the development of conscience, cause-and-effect thinking, logic and empathy.

Attachment history A child's history of significant relationships and the security, or lack of security, safety, or lack of safety, of those relationships with parents, wider family, carers or adopters. It may also include other significant individuals including teachers or even pets. Any type of trauma and loss is especially important to note, even if a loss had been deemed to be in the best interest of the child (for example, loss of contact with an abusive parent): as is any kind of extraordinary stress experienced. We need to know what they have lived through from pregnancy onwards, if there has been any kind of potential disruption to the usual bonding/attachment process.

The Key Adult in School

Attachment Lead An Attachment Lead is an appointed and trained member of staff in the school who seeks to lead the way in attachment awareness and trauma informed interventions and embed them into policy on behalf of troubled pupils. This is usually a member of support staff on the ground leading through practice with individual pupils, and a member of Senior Management leading through advocacy and strategic action amongst the whole school community. See attachmentleadnetwork.net for more information on the training required.

Attachment system An innate urge within humans (and other mammals) that impels us to seek promixity to and relationship with others. Attachment serves two important functions: a protective function and a secure base effect. It is in our interest to stay close to another person, especially when we are very young, defenceless and vulnerable. Staying close can keep us safe. It is also in our interest to have someone to act as our secure base. If we have a secure base, we are then freed up to set off out of our comfort zone into the unfamiliar, the unknown, into unchartered territory - the world is ours to learn. We can do this knowing that we can return to our secure base before venturing off again. Our secure base gives us the confidence we need in order to take the risks required in learning. Our attachment system (of neural connections and hormone release leading to attachment seeking behaviour) is activated if we experience anxiety.

Developmental Trauma A term used by Van der Kolk (2014) and many other attachment aware and trauma informed practitioners to describe a child's experiences of repeated or prolonged trauma through neglect, abuse, abandonment, violence, loss, parental substance misuse or addiction. Developmental trauma implies that the child's developing brain will have been impacted, with negative effects on the development of their executive functions, motor skills, and capacity to self-regulate, communicate and relate. Left unattended at home and/or in school, the effects of developmental trauma are likely to persist into adulthood and have profound effects on every aspect of the individual's life.

Developmental vulnerability A term that can sometimes be used in schools to describe children whose emotional and social development has been adversely affected by relational trauma and loss. Many of these children can experience emotional, cognitive, physical and social delays, and present as much younger than their chronological age. Their development can also be impaired due to what they have experienced in their short lives to date. It is sometimes helpful to use as a descriptor in schools so that these pupils are not at risk of being misunderstood. Education staff will use very different strategies to address difficulties in these instances. There is the possibility of adaption and even recovery from extraordinary stress with the right kind of help.

Disrupted relationships/connections Relationships and connections that have been disrupted or compromised for the individual child through having early experiences of loss, abuse, neglect, trauma, domestic violence, or parental substance abuse or mental ill health. Disruption isn't necessarily intentional (although it can be) but can come about due to circumstance: for example, medical complications at birth, having a mother who becomes unwell after birth … the ordinary development of brain connections may have been disrupted if these experiences happen at certain crucial times, or for prolonged periods. Disruptions often compromise or disrupt trust. There are many children in our care who have experienced intimacy betrayals at the hands of their own birth parents. The deep distrust that has been created out of relational experience is then often projected onto other adults, regardless of their intentions or motives. We can in fact get caught up in their time-warp, experiencing the distress, grief and rage intended for someone else, in another time and place.

The Key Adult in School

Exploratory system An innate urge within humans (and other mammals) that impels us to explore, experiment, play, and thereby learn. The exploratory system (of neural connections and hormone release leading to exploratory behaviour) is activated or reaches its full potential when the attachment system is well attended to. If the attachment system is not attended to, the exploratory system (which is needed for learning) will be impeded by ongoing anxiety.

Fight/flight/freeze response The range of responses we produce in relation to threat or perceived threat. Physiological, cognitive and emotional effects are triggered by the release of stress hormones. Each individual's most likely pattern of response is experience dependent. The pattern can be modified over time (*and see* p.51).

Insecure attachment This indicates a level of insecurity that interferes with the child's ability to relate in a healthy or appropriate way to other people. Such insecurity arose from early uncertainties about the reliability of his or her parent or primary carer. We can observe too much dependence or too much independence in his response to his needs and the satisfaction of those needs. There are traditionally three main types of insecure attachment, sometimes described as avoidant, ambivalent and disorganised.

Intersubjective experience The experience created between two individuals, for example an adult and child, by sharing communication, affect, meaning, and their sense of themselves and of eachother as what is happening between them unfolds. We learn who we are through the minds and hearts of others. Relates to 'mind-mindedness'.

Regulatory system If we have received consistent and sufficient regulatory experiences ourselves, through being received by calming and soothing others, especially in our early years, then we are more able to internalise what becomes our own regulatory system (internal and external tools and strategies) to help us self-regulate at times of stress. If, however, we haven't had appropriate calming and soothing, at the right time, then our regulatory systems can be over-active and we can end up becoming dysregulated very frequently, even for everyday ordinary stressors. This is why many of our pupils need so much help with regulation.

Relational buffering Rich relational connection serves a protective function. It provides protection from the full impact of stress. It prevents stress from becoming toxic and damaging us. Those who have experienced relational poverty/withdrawal or trauma are very vulnerable and fragile in the midst of everyday ordinary stressors, as well as extraordinary toxic stressors. This puts them at further risk.

Many of the pupils in our care who have experienced significant relational trauma and loss had to manage big overwhelming states, sensations and feelings on their own. Because this occurred when their developing nervous systems were very fragile, they have learned to rely on their feeling brain, their limbic system (that is now very well developed) in relation to stressors that come their way.

If we can now stand in the gap and give these pupils the sensitive, attuned care that they didn't have or didn't have enough of in their early years, then we are in effect providing them with the relational buffering they need in order to interrupt the impulsivity that occurs by using the emotional brain in isolation. We can in effect become like 'external brains', lending them our thinking brain to inhibit impulsivity, until they can manage for themselves. Check out the 'handbrain model' on Youtube, by Daniel Siegel.

Relational trauma Trauma experienced by the child on a repeated basis within the context of relationship (often from within early attachments) eg abuse, neglect, violence, intrusion, loss, abandonment and so on. The child may well have experienced overwhelm, powerlessness and terror in

The Key Adult in School

the process. The child may well now be completely confused as to the role and purpose of adults, having experienced such overwhelm in their care. It is not surprising therefore that coming into contact with us is going to mean them moving into pseudo-independent states, however caring we may try to be.

Relative dependency This term describes what we may be able to facilitate in schools, in order to give a child who has experienced early relational trauma and loss an opportunity for learning, trust and security through the relationship with a consistent adult who offers sensitive care: in this case, the **Key Adult**.

Secure attachment This indicates a healthy and appropriate style of relating to other people. An interplay of dependence and independence is observed in response to needs and the satisfaction of those needs.

Toxic stress We all experience ordinary stressors in life. However if a child with a fragile and developing nervous system experiences extraordinary stressors, for example at the hands of his or her own parents, over a period of time, then the child can move into overwhelm. This overwhelm, which can include being flooded with high levels of stress hormones for significant periods, can put undue pressure on the developing body and brain, heart and mind, meaning that their natural development and functioning may become disrupted. This may lead to the state described as 'developmental vulnerability', or trauma.

Wounded self (fragile, vulnerable) The part of him or herself the child has unconsciously 'buried' or hidden in order to survive unbearable stress in situations of relational trauma and loss (Taransaud 2011).

Window of stress tolerance see p.48

References

Aspden, K.L. (2015) *Help! I've got an alarm bell going off in my head! How panic, anxiety and stress affect your body* London: Jessica Kingsley Publishers

Belsky, J., Vandell, D.L., Burchinal, M., Clarke-Stewart, K.A., McCartney, K., Owen, M.P. & The NICHD Early Child Care Research Network (2007) Are There Long-Term Effects of Early Child Care? *Child Development* Vol 78, (2)pp.681-701

Bombèr, L.M. (2007) *Inside I'm Hurting: Practical strategies for supporting children with attachment difficulties in schools* London: Worth Publishing

Bombèr, L.M. (2009) Survival of the fittest: teenagers finding their way through the labyrinth of transitions in schools *in*, Perry, A. (Ed.) *Teenagers and Attachment: Helping adolescents engage with life and learning* London: Worth Publishing

Bombèr, L.M. (2011) *What About Me? Inclusive strategies to support pupils with attachment difficulties make it through the school day* London: Worth Publishing

Bombèr, L.M. & Hughes, D. (2013) *Settling to Learn: Why relationships matter in schools* London: Worth Publishing

Bombèr, L.M. (2015) *The Key Adult in School, Attachment Aware School Series Book 1* Duffield, Derbyshire: Worth Publishing

Bombèr, L.M. (2016) *The Senior Manager in School, Attachment Aware School Series Book 2* Duffield, Derbyshire: Worth Publishing

Bombèr, L.M. (2016) *The Key Teacher in School, Attachment Aware School Series Book 3* Duffield, Derbyshire: Worth Publishing

The Key Adult in School

Bombèr, L.M. (2016) *Team Pupil in School, Attachment Aware School Series Book 4* Duffield, Derbyshire: Worth Publishing

Bombèr, L.M. (2016) *The Parent and Carer in School, Attachment Aware School Series Book 5* Duffield, Derbyshire: Worth Publishing

Booth, P. & Jernberg, A. (2010) *Theraplay: Helping parents and children build better relationships through attachment based play* New York: John Wiley & Sons

Brown, B. (2012) *Daring Greatly: How the courage to be vulnerable transforms the way we live, love, parent and lead* London: Penguin Books Ltd

Brown, B. (2010) *Ted Talk on Vulnerability* ted.com/talks/brene_brown_on_vulnerability?language=en

Cameron, C., Connelly, G. & Jackson, S. (2015) *Educating Children and Young People in Care* London: Jessica Kingsley

Circle of Security youtube clip youtube.com/watch?v=F6DhnbgRAOo Shark Music vimeo.com/145329119

Clarke, J. & Dawson, C. (1998) *Growing Up Again* Minnesota, USA: Hazelden

Cozolino, L. (2013) *The Social Neuroscience of Education:Optimizing attachment and learning in the classroom* New York: WW Norton

Cozolino, L. (2014) *The Neuroscience of Human Relationships: A practical guide for the inner journey* New York: WW Norton

Forbes, H. (2011) *Overwhelm - Beyond Consequences: Parenting Solutions* Youtube v=X9zLKSoYOaO

Forbes, H. (2012) *Help for Billy: A Beyond Consequences approach to helping challenging children in the classroom* Beyond Consequences Institute, LLC. beyondconsequences.com

Geddes, H. (2006) *Attachment in the Classroom* London: Worth Publishing

Golding, K.S. (2007) *Nurturing Attachments. Supporting children who are fostered or adopted.* London, Jessica Kingsley

Golding, K.S., Fain, J., Frost, A., Mills, C., Worrall, H., Roberts, N., Durant, E. & Templeton, S. (2012) *Observing Children with Attachment Difficulties in School: A tool for identifying and supporting emotional and social difficulties in children* London: Jessica Kingsley

Golding, K.S. & Hughes, D. (2012) *Creating Loving Attachments* London: Jessica Kingsley

Golding, K.S. (2013) *Nurturing Attachments Training Resource. Running parenting groups for adoptive parents and foster or kinship carers.* London, Jessica Kingsley

Golding, K.S. (2014) *Using Stories to Build Bridges with Traumatised Children* London: Jessica Kingsley

Greenhalgh, P. (1994) *Emotional Growth & Learning* London: Routledge

Gregory, A. & Weinstein, R.S. (2004) Connection and Regulation at Home and in School: Predicting growth in achievement for adolescents *Journal of Adolescent Research* July, Vol 19 (4) pp.405-427

Handford, M. (2104) *Where's Wally?* books UK: Walker Books

Hughes, D. (2004) *Facilitating Developmental Attachment: The road to emotional recovery and behavioural change in foster and adopted children* Maryland, USA: Aronson Inc

Hughes, D. (2009) *Principles of Attachment-Focused Parenting: Effective strategies to care for children* London: WW Norton

Hughes, D. (2013) *8 Keys to Building your Best Relationships* New York: WW Norton

Hughes, D. & Baylin, J. (2012) *Brain-Based Parenting: The neuroscience of caregiving for healthy attachment* New York: WW Norton

Hughes, D. (2016) Attachment Conference London: Centre for Child Mental Health, (April)

Johnstone, M. (2012) *Quiet the Mind* London: Robinson

Karst, P. (2000) *The Invisible String* Camarilla, CA: Devorss & Co

Kintsugi youtube.com/watch?v=EBUTQkaSSTY
youtube.com/watch?v=IT55_u8URU0

The Key Adult in School

Magorian, M. (2014) *Goodnight Mr Tom* London: Puffin Classic

Maté, G. (2013) *Attachment and Brain Development*
 YouTube/v=UbiWLLYSZhc

Mayo Clinic mayoclinic.org/healthy-lifestyle/stress-management/in-depth/stress-relief/art-20044456?pg=1

Meyer, J (2016) *Overload: How to unplug, unwind and free yourself from the pressure of stress* London: Hodder & Stoughton

Music, G. (2011) *Nurturing Natures: Attachment and children's emotional, sociocultural and brain development* Hove: Psychology Press

Music, G. (2014) *The Good Life: Wellbeing and the new science of altruism, selfishness and immorality* Hove, UK: Routledge

Olson, K. (2014) *The Invisible Classroom: Relationships, neuroscience & mindfulness in school* New York: WW Norton

Palmer, S. (2007) *Toxic Childhood* London: Orion

Perry, B. (1999) *Memories of Fear: How the brain stores and retrieves physiologic states, feelings, behaviours and thoughts from traumatic events* Academy version, The Child Trauma Academy Houston, Texas
 childtrauma.org/wp-content/uploads/2014/12/Memories_of_Fear_Perry.pdf

Perry, B. (2010) *Born for Love: Why empathy is essential and endangered* New York: Harper Collins Publishers

Perry, B. (2014) *Brain Development and Learning*
 Columbus Metropolitan Club, Youtube/DXdBFFph2QQ

Powell, B., Cooper, G., Hoffman, K. & Marvin, R. (2013) *The Circle of Security Intervention: Enhancing attachment in early parent-child relationships* New York: Guildford Press

Riley, P. (2011) *Attachment Theory and the Teacher-Student Relationship: A practical guide for teachers, teacher educators and school leaders* Oxon: Routledge

Robinson, K. (2010) *The Element: How finding your passion changes everything* UK: Penguin

Siegel, D. (1999) *The Developing Mind* New York: The Guildford Press
Siegel, D. (2012) The Hand Model of the Brain

youtube.com/watch?v=gm9ClJ74Oxw

Siegel, D. & Bryson, T.P. (2012) *The Whole Brain Child: 12 proven strategies to nurture your child's developing mind* London: Robinson

Siegel, D. & Bryson, T.P. (2014) *No-Drama Discipline: The whole brain way to calm the chaos and nurture your child's developing mind* Australia & UK: Scribe

Siegel, D.J. & Bryson, T.P. (2015) *Connect and Redirect Refrigerator Sheet*
drdansiegel.com/pdf/Refrigerator%20Sheet--NDD.pdf

Street, K. (2014) *School as a Secure Base: How peaceful teachers can create peaceful schools* London: Worth Publishing

Sunderland, M. (2006) *The Science of Parenting: Practical guidance on sleep, crying, play and building emotional wellbeing for life* London: Dorling Kindersley

Sunderland, M. (2015) *Conversations that Matter: Talking with children and teenagers in ways that help* Derbyshire, UK: Worth Publishing

Sunderland, M. (2016) *Best Relationship with your Child* DVD Series
childmentalhealthcentre.org/buy-dvds/category

Taransaud, D. (2011) *You Think I'm Evil: Practical strategies for working with aggressive and rebellious adolescents* London: Worth Publishing

Thierry, B. (2015) *Teaching the Child on the Trauma Continuum* Surrey: Grosvenor House Publishing Ltd

Van der Kolk, B. (2014) *The Body Keeps the Score: Brain, mind and body in the healing of trauma* New York, US: Viking

Wetz, J. (2009) *Urban Village Schools: Putting relationships at the heart of secondary school organisation and design* UK: Calouste Gulbenkian Foundation

Wilson, D. & Newton, C. (2006) *Circle of Adults: A team approach to problem solving around challenging behaviour and emotional needs* Nottingham: Inclusive solutions

WiseUp! adoptionsupport.org/
store/w-i-s-e-up-powerbook-for-children-in-foster-care

The Key Adult in School
Useful contacts

Attachment Lead Network	attachmentleadnetwork.net
B.A.S.E.® Babywatching UK	base-babywatching-uk.org
Beyond Consequences	beyondconsequences.com
Bruce D. Perry, Psychiatrist	childtrauma.org
Caspari Foundation	caspari.org.uk
Centre for Child Mental Health	childmentalhealthcentre.org
The Centre for Emotional Development	emotionaldevelopment.co.uk
Child Trauma Academy	childtrauma.org
Circle of Security	circleofsecurity.net
Consortium for Emotional Well Being in Schools	jameswetz3@gmail.com
Daniel A. Hughes, Child Psychologist	danielhughes.org

Dan Siegel, Professor of Psychiatry	drdansiegel.com
Dyadic Development Psychotherapy UK	ddpnetwork.org/uk
Heart Math	heartmath.com
Inclusive Solutions	inclusive-solutions.com
Institute for Arts in Therapy and Education London	artspsychotherapy.org
Institute for Recovery from Childhood Trauma	irct.org.uk
Nurture Group Network	nurturegroups.org
Pets as Therapy	petsastherapy.org
Theraplay®	theraplay.org
Transforming Lives for Good	tlg.org.uk

The Key Adult in School